Increased Risk

For my mother,
whose belief in me decreased every risk

Table of Contents

SAD

ANGRY

HOPEFUL

SAD

I Greet the World In Pain

I greet the world
in pain
or not at all—

so I greet the world in pain.

Daisy Chains

My pain started
in little girl days
when my friends and I developed code words
for when I didn't feel good
and my mom sat holding my hand
in every waiting room.

I was wild and undiscoverable,
placed in antiseptic rooms
where I was measured and told
to fit.

It was the kind of pain you learn
to grow around.

This is the world, and you enter it
unsuspecting,
a thorn in your side
and chains of daisies
braided into your hair.

For the Undiagnosed:

This is the worst it will ever get.

Nothing compares to the agony
of not knowing what is going on
in your own body.

This is the temporary part.
The part you just have to live through.

The Weight

For the first half of my life
my failing body
felt like my mother's problem.
It was hardly any of my business.

She was the one to research doctors
and book appointments,
to keep track of medicines
and reason with teachers about why
I should be allowed to move on to the next grade
when I wasn't at school half the week,
all while I wept from the foot of my bed
that none of it was helping.

Everyone else in my family
had to bear witness to my pain,
but I expected my mother
to fix it.

So on she went fighting battles
that she didn't feel and couldn't name.
I ate what I was told to
and peed into the cups that I was told to
and complained every moment of it.
"Mommy," I would say, my heart in my throat,
"something's wrong. Something hurts."

Math problems, she was prepared for.
A failed test, an attitude problem,
the eventual romantic troubles. But this?
None of us knew how to navigate it.

It never felt insurmountable
until I was living on my own trying to manage it
mostly by myself.
Only then did I understand the luxury
of having every decision made for me.

The first doctor's appointment
I went to alone
I felt hollow. When asked about my medical history
I said, "hang on, let me text my mom."

My mother, with two children to raise
and a stressful job and the usual pressures
of pulling me into adulthood
kind and functioning and smart.
My mother,
with my health
in the palm of her hand.

Even now
we carry it between us.
How did she ever manage the weight of it herself?

Diagnosis

I sat on the examining table,
so small,
and made big choices about my future:

When to start the medicines
I'm still on
ten years later.
Ones that slowly gave me cancer
and my entire life back.

Increased Risk

Take the pills
that render your immune system useless;
it's better than it was before. Useless
is better than poised to attack you,
a body bent on hurting its own self,
so dangerous we put it in restraints
and leave you open to whatever wandering infection
may take up the fight against you.
This is how you get better:
by getting worse.
By getting everything
that floats through the air
or lives on a surface
or passes over someone
with a body that works better than yours.
Get better by getting
long lists of side effects,
words that doctors whisper
at the end of each injection.
Get your moles checked twice a year,
get over your fear of needles and get every vaccine.
You're probably fine,
you're just at an increased risk.
Sometimes I feel like my whole life
is an increased risk. A clawing, constant battle
to be healthy like everyone else is most of the time.
A very delicate balance
that I can slip onto either side of
and end up back in a hospital bed.

Some days I want what other people have.
Some days I want the worst of it to happen,
just so it stops hanging over my head.
Most days I just want my sore throat to go away.
It's back again,
a minor annoyance,
a reminder of the things I try
to escape.

The Lonely Thing About It

Here's the lonely thing about it: they rally around you at first. That first night you spend in the hospital freaks everyone out. Gets their attention. They call, text, check up on you. But then your appointments become scheduled. There aren't anymore ambulances, just silent car rides with worried parents. You don't flinch when they get the needles out anymore. Friends stop calling to see how you are. And stop bringing flowers. And once sitting around with you gets dull they decide to go out instead. They go on hikes, and see shows, and go to parties. You'll watch movies from your bed where protagonists will go on hikes and see shows and go to parties. You will smile for your mother and take your temperature every ten minutes. You will starve yourself for a day so they can stick a camera down your throat. Everyone will want to know the color of your urine. You will be too tired to go out- you will be called lazy. It's okay to feel too sick to go out with your friends, but it's not okay to go to bed early instead of doing your homework. Your friends will stay in with you. The guilt will be worse than the loneliness. You will call yourself blessed. You will comfort your mother. You will try not to cry when she calls you to chat, but you will. She will cry when you hang up. Your peers will call you lazy. You will thank your friends for their prayers. You will learn to say "it's okay," a thousand different ways. You will drive home for an appointment. You will drive back for class. You will not get to eat. You will drive home for surgery. You will sleep through the weekend. You will drive back for class.

You will do your homework early so you can sleep through your evening fever. You will tell your mom you are fine and then you will cry in the bath. You will call your friend in the middle of the night and ask for a story—anything, something happy just to get your mind off of all of this. He will make you laugh. You will cry tears of joy for it. He will hang up and go back to his healthy life. And then you will be alone. Repeat.

Battleground

My body and I are always at war
but I'm trying to make peace.

I take it to the doctor and
I feed it things it needs and still
it makes me sick like a taunt.

"I have power over you,"
it says when I call out from work again
or cry on the way to the clinic
or crawl back into my bed.

"Listen, please, I'm hurting,"
is what I think it really means.

My body and I are often
on opposite sides of the fight,
but I'm learning to love it anyway.

I dress it the way I like
and make my hair the color
I always wanted and still,
I look into the mirror
and my eyes fix first on what I dislike.

"I have power over you,"
I tell it when the hateful thoughts
creep into my head.

I am the person
and you are just the body—
you don't get a say in how I feel about myself.

But "listen, please, I'm hurting," feels more right.

Sales Tax

What a humbling gift
you have been given,
the reminder that a body
is more
than the way it looks.

For a while the idea of a good body
will just be having a body
that works.

What a gift.

And what a price to pay.

Half-life

When I am in pain
I am only half of myself.
The other half
taken up by hurt.

My brain works
in half-time.

I am talking to you
but my words
come
out
dripping, colored red.

And then I halve the half—
you see, it takes that much effort
to act like I'm not in pain.

So I am a quarter of myself.

The rest has gone to hurting
and pretending not to hurt.

When you speak
the words filter through the claws
and come into my head in ribbons.

I piece them back together
and send my own
out through the grinder.

This part takes a third
of what remains,
so really,
there is so little
of me
left.

The Never Ending Fight

Some days
I think
I might dislike
the chronic part
more than the illness part.

Ouroboros

Having Crohn's disease
felt at first like having Crohn's disease
and then briefly, after medication,
like being healthy, and then mostly
like just catching everything else.

I am eating my own tail,
taking pills that keep me healthy
and leave me hanging, waiting
out whatever infection I had been
the bait for.

A bit double-edged, this
miracle I prayed for.

Foundation

When the migraines came
they came from behind,
gripping the back of my skull
and wrapping long fingers
around to my temples.

It is not instantaneous.
They creep in
like a thought.
Something I was meant to remember;
oh yes,
I am a girl in pain.

They took everything
in pieces.
My spontaneity,
my easy way of being,
some favorite foods and drinks,
and the subject of so many conversations
that I often wonder what else it was
I would've talked about
had this never happened to me at all.

Now I miss not
tapering down
each experience
to be just tolerable
enough.

It's such a strange thing to describe,
how I've lived through difficult things
but chronic pain has undone me so completely.

I don't know how else to say it
but that it's always there now,
holding court, making little changes
to everything I thought was fundamental.

Something To Keep

My partner is at the pharmacy right now
picking up my prescription.
We fought about it
but just a little.

He doesn't want me to go and get sicker
but I don't want to feel like a burden
which lately I always do
and it seems like there's no helping it.

Neither of us blames the other
but there's a lot of frustration
and nowhere for it to go.
It makes my headaches worse just thinking about it.

This is the new pill
which is actually the old pill
that I threw out when it wasn't working
and they prescribed me the new one
which is now the old one.
It's not until he gets there that I realize
if I hadn't thrown it out
we could've avoided this whole thing.

I have had a headache for three years now.
Apparently that's a thing that can just happen.
I really miss waking up to a headache and thinking
"this'll clear up by lunch." Still.

I have a person that I love
to fight with about if I am too much work
to take care of.
But my head hurts.
Just something to keep in mind.

Worthy

How to believe it's your choice
when I watch you put me first?

How do I ask for more from people
than I'm scared
I'm worth?

On Being Used to It:

"Does it hurt,
or are you used to it?"
is something that my partner
asks me often. It's sad
or it's lovely, depending how you look at it.
"How's your head?" he asks gently.
"Any better? Or did you just get used to it?"
I contemplate the answer.
"Maybe a little less bad," I'll say,
and I know he takes my words to heart.
It's something he once told me
he loves about me,
that I tell the truth
about how I feel.
I'd never thought of it like that, but now
it makes me laugh. I've always been a whiner.
And here is this perfect person,
a person I've always imagined,
who says to me
"I love that you tell the truth about how you feel."
It's so lucky that it feels silly.
Most people in my life
are good with my pain.
Patient and understanding.
I don't leave much room for any other option.
But there's something about his question
that feels different.
Does it hurt, or are you just used to it?

It implies that I am tough,
which I like. It makes me feel brave and strong
instead of weak. And it's loving,
of course it is.
It's being remembered
in the middle of a fun time.
But why does it cut right to my heart?
Does it hurt, or are you just used to it?
You see that, how in both of the options
he believes I'm still in pain?
He doesn't doubt it
just because I smiled.
He doesn't say, oh, I can tell you feel better!
He doesn't have to ask me
if it's still there.

He believed me the first time.

Thin Ice

The worst part
of leaning on someone else
is the moment you notice
you've gotten too heavy.

Carry Me

There are some weaknesses
you can only give over to a mother.
I need so much help
with the body you created.
Carry me, so I don't have to be alone.

Partly Cloudy

Some people wake up healthy.
Some people wake up to endless red tape
and hoops to jump through
just to have the chance to feel close to that.

I've always wondered what it would be like to say
"at least I have my health."
To not have your own weakness
hanging like a cloud over your head.

It doesn't always rain,
but you never fully see the sun.

This Is Me in Remission?

Even when everything's perfect,
everything's wrong?

Vanishing Act

I am typing this through squinted eyes
on lowest brightness before I fall asleep
in pain.
It used to be living
with moments of pain
blooming bright and hot in between,
but now there is only
going to sleep in pain
and waking up in pain
and the rush to get your work done
before the worst of it sets in.
The things I love are laced with it.
A cap is low on my head
against the overhead lights.
My temper is short.
I have always valued my good spirits
in the face of suffering;
I have always thought myself a good patient.
Once I'm better I'll have to ask everyone else
if they think the same.
Have you ever gone to sleep in pain
and woken up in pain?
Have you ever told yourself
it will be better in the morning
knowing full well
it's just a quicker way to get to sleep?
Have you faced the hurt that won't be solved
the next day or the next month or the next;

have you stood in front of something and known
it would be a long long way until you stopped feeling it?
I tell myself it won't last
when I know it will. I tell myself it won't come back
when it always has. I tell myself
it'll be solved by next year
and then next year is now
and I'm gritting my teeth
writing this.
Chronic is just a word they give you
that means find a way to live with it. And we do.
And sometimes the world forgets
because we get good at making them more comfortable.
Sometimes I mention it just so someone else will know.
I am in physical pain
more often than I am without it.
It's that way for a lot of us.
More people than you'd think.
And everyone always asks me what they can do to help.
I don't know, other than this. Just listen.
Just let me be in pain
and be everything else I am.
Don't make me hide it.
It takes everything
just to endure it.
Don't make me hide it, too.

Placeholder

I didn't want to be the girl
with migraines.
No one who has them does.

The one who sits out
when everyone else goes on the rollercoaster—
just in case.

The one who can't have a drink
by the pool
in the middle of the afternoon anymore.

The one who can't run too fast
or sing along to the music
if it's too loud
or leave her house
without three different kinds of pain relief.

I can't go to the movies without headphones.
I never wanted to be that girl.

And everyone says
that I wouldn't be me
if I didn't have to go through what I've been through,
but what if I felt more like me before?

What if I actually am the rollercoaster girl
and I was forced by circumstance
to unlearn her?

The conversation always comes back
to strength.
It's made you strong, you're just so strong.

And I am! It's true.
But I wish I didn't have to be.

Sometimes I feel like I'm strong
in place of all the other things
I used to be.

Just Fine

On Monday my doctor called me
with some words I had been dreading
for weeks now,
ones I always know are coming
after too long without an answer:

you're fine.

There's always this
weird pause
when I don't react happily to the good news.
It's strange when you know it could be worse,
but you were still hoping for something better.

The Weather

It creeps up
very
slowly.
That's the problem
with pain. I only ever notice
that I was pain free
once it comes back
again.

The absence of it isn't enough for me—
it always takes the return of it
for me to realize how good I had it.

It's like if someone
took a screwdriver to my jaw
or my temple
but they were invisible
and I still had to
run errands
and go vote
and meet my friends for dinner
and maybe someone will notice
a look in my eye
and ask the silent question
and I'll squeeze your hand
and nod; yes, I am in pain.

Everything I say or do
for the foreseeable future is alongside it.

Pain and I are tangled up.

You call it the weather.
We can try to predict the forecast
but some days when you wake up it's raining,
and whatever the plan was
you adjust.
There's nothing to do
but deal with it.
It's out of my hands.
It's the weather.

And I have rainy day plans.
Appointments
and pills
and procedures
and lots and lots of hope.

But I miss the feeling of walking out into the sunshine,
worried about everything but
an umbrella.

Bitter Pill

You slide the medicine
across the table
toward me. "Do you want to take it now?"

I'm slumped forward
on the couch, cracked in half
at the waist. My hands are a vice
around my skull. I shake my head.

"Are you sure?" you press.
"The doctor said three times a week
and you've only done Friday
so you have two more days.
No? Okay."

I save my pain away.
I'm always counting on a worse day.

The next day I make an excuse.
I don't want to feel sleepy.
I was hoping to get some work done.

A day later
when the pain is ripping through my jaw
you lay the medicine out in front of me
and I tell you I want to wait until later.
Later, my feet in your lap,
you call me on my shit.

"It's Tuesday," you say. "You can take it.
Why don't you want to?"

I don't know how to say
I'm in control of so little.
It makes me feel better just knowing it's there.
I like the idea that I didn't need to use it,
that if it gets unbearable
there's always something that can help.
And taking it feels a little
like admitting defeat.

But my head hurts so badly
I can barely string those thoughts together.
And that feels like a sign enough.
I swallow my pride
and the medicine
at once.

Thief

My migraines are stealing my memories.
They're taking my important moments.
I wanted that day! I want it back!
I dreamed about it for years
and now it's foggy.
Thief.
That mattered so much to me.

And no one but me
knows how deep I have to reach
to pull through it.
They can imagine, but only I know the extent.
I feel it when I wake up in the morning:
if I'm capable of trying.

If I'm capable of being two separate people—
the one that's needed
and the one that hurts.
I was both, for days on end.
Weeks and weeks on end.
Every morning you step carefully out of your house,
praying that the ground is solid.
You never know.
At any moment everything could slip.

And it's made me superstitious,
if I wasn't already. It's made me religious.
I pray

and count
and knock on wood
and hold my breath
and stretch and follow all the rules.
I worry and bargain— not that day, take this one.
And I can do it but I won't be me,
I wish I could explain, how I'm not strong enough
and so I go away and the thing that takes my place is
cold and invincible.
Being someone else is what I'm best at.
It's a cultivated skill,
being alive and in pain.
The part that no one but him will ever see:
me, curled inward, forehead to the bathroom tile
in a silent prayer,
sobbing until the sound is all gone.
Choking out the words:
"It's ruined my life. It took everything from me."
To look into the eyes of the person
who loves you most in the world
and still feel so lonely.
To be trapped in a body that's in pain,
a layer of glass between you
even when you're lying next to each other in bed.
My head is on his shoulder in one world,
the one where I'm safe.
But my head is also on fire.

I get so tired of putting it out.

Little Pains

Every summer
you get one really bad sunburn.
Every winter, right around Christmas,
you gain a little bit of weight.
Your hair grows longer
and you usually let it.
Your nails grow longer
until one of them breaks
and then you cut them all short.
At least twice a year
you'll get a really bad cold
that keeps you down and out for a while.
In the spring your skin dries out,
your lips will chap,
your knuckles crack.

These are some of the ways that your body helps
and fails you. Every year, trusted,
like clock-work. Dependable.
They are inevitabilities
that you come to count on.

There is one thing
that you can't count on.

Your medicine has stopped working.
You are no longer in remission.

And you've always known it would happen.
It's the nature of a cyclical disease.
But still.

It hurts a little worse
than a sunburn.

The Prayer

Every one of my mornings starts with medication.
Just two pills, not particularly difficult to swallow.

I reach a hand out of my blanket
and fumble for them
the way healthy people search for the snooze button.
And it doesn't hurt me to do it, just reminds me.
I am sick. I always will be.

Some people pray, I think.
Or stretch their bodies to get a feel for the morning.
And I lay my life at the altar of two tiny white pills:
please keep my organs going, please save my life.

It is a little ritual.
The sound, the screwing of the lid,
the taste of talc and hopefulness.

I am sick and I always will be, but today I'll save my life.

And then and only then I am free to be a person
like any other.
To press the snooze, to check my phone.
To pray for whatever else I'd like to pray for.

But still, it is my first and only thought every morning.

Before I am a person I am a body failing.
I am a body trying hard to live at all.

Mundanity

So much of chronic illness
becomes mundane.
You stop by the hospital
on your way home from work.
You dress your wounds
in front of the tv.

But every once in a while I remember
that it's a lot.
It's a lot.

And some people
don't have to do it
just to live.

Invisible

All your life people will tell you
that you are sick
but you're not sick enough for it to matter.

When your illness is invisible
you're all risk
and no reward.
Who would pat them on the back
if they hire you? Who would even know?

And so you play the part of sick person
in the hospital
but normal person outside of it.
No one wants to hear anything else from you.
You tell them about your illness and they say
"wow, I would never know," and you think
"good? I've done it?" and also
"I wish you would."

Even friendly faces forget
and you wonder if it's your job to remind them
or your job to smile through it.
Which version are you being today?

Sometimes it's a super power;
you get moments from strangers
that someone who couldn't hide it would never get.
You can stand next to healthy people
and no one questions that you're one of them.

And you're glad until they expect the same from you
and you can't give it.

No one knows how much work it takes,
pretending that you're one of them.
How many pills are in your backpack
to cover the exhaustion of maintaining
your healthy face.

Take this one when you're home, the doctor says,
but save this one for when you have to
get through the day.
You are an expert at getting through the day.

There are consolations.
Best friends who know your tells:
the blank stare, when your hand tenses up
in the middle of a movement, when you go quiet
at a time you would've once been loud.

They are there to remind you
that when you succeed it means more.
You are no better or worse,
no more deserving,
but it means more.

Anniversary

Thirty years
in a body
that feels more like a job.

Limits and Proofs

Life becomes very very small—
everything boiled down to
the next moment of relief.

If I don't talk about it
will they think I don't feel it?
 If I smile will they say
"looks like you're feeling better!"

How to give the world its proof
that I'm hurting
and still let myself feel happy?

The Same Twenty-four

Sometimes it feels like I only have time
for one thing
before the migraine
descends
and sends me back to bed again.
The hours shrink.
The days and weeks shrink, too.
All that time you thought you had
stretching out before you,
and what will you do with it?
Exercise? Do the dishes?
Catch up on emails?
See a friend?
Drive yourself to a doctor's appointment?

Today you just write this.

And you look back over the months
and there's no progress.
Only constant struggle
to stay in the exact same spot.
Only countless hours
alone in the dark, trying to soothe
the one thing that always demands your attention.
Please, can I have some of it back?
Can I borrow it, just for an hour,
just to do something that I like? Just to do my laundry?
Sometimes I look at my life
and think I'd like to do more.

Am I losing something? Am I wasting it?
Sometimes I look at my life
and think I'm trying to do too much.
Shouldn't I plan around my pain?
Shouldn't I make things as easy on myself as possible?
What's the line between giving up
and self care? What's the line between being young
and sick?
They say we all have the same twenty-four hours
in our day.
Is it really that many? Twenty-four seems like a luxury.
At this point I'll settle for two.

Before and After

Chronic Pain has ruined me like this: everyone I love still loves me. Everyone is safe. I'm still in the middle of my dream life. Most days I'm happy. But everything— every little thing— has been made worse.

I care for my migraines like they're something I have to love. I never leave the house without packing their bag. I take them to the doctor twice a month. I submit my body to them. I give them attention, lie down with them, listen to them, heed them. I've changed my routine, changed my diet, changed my face.

Constant pain has overhauled my life in ways I will never be able to put into words. If you've felt it you know, and you are irrevocably different from the person you were before you knew.

I've come to treasure my hardships. I find they make me soft in a way I like. I find they've opened my arms to strangers instead of closing them.

But this? I would give anything to change it. Change me, make me back into the person I was before. For all the ways I've been made better, I'd give it all back in an instant to not wake up and wonder if I'll have a day without pain.

*Because I Went Too Long
Before Someone Told Me:*

You are not dispensable.

A Great Life in Glimpses

This isn't how I pictured my life.
I found the guy. I chased the dream.
Made my home on a street lined with palm trees.
I planned ahead. I thought it through.
But I never thought of this.

Each morning spent waking up in pain—
scared to see just how much.
Each event spent dodging pain—
what cocktail of meds and stretches can I do
to give myself a normal hour?
How do I get myself through a thing
I have to do? And worse— how do I enjoy it?

All the things I said I needed to be happy
piled at my feet, and I enjoy them in glimpses.
I breathe air like the rest of them
before I'm pulled back under.
Then it's hours spent fighting
for thirty minutes of peace.

And I forget— I forget.
Life gets cluttered with plans.
There's no anticipating this. You can try
and you can pack the tools and stay on the phone
with CVS
and order shots to a pharmacy another other coast—
you can try.

But in the end you will be living your dream life
in slivers.
You will watch the good years rushing past you
from your bed.
No responsibilities, young and in love,
you should be on planes right now.
You should be dancing on no sleep.
You are in the waiting room,
he's holding your hand.

Your pain takes you from romance
to partnership
so fast
you get whiplash.
I guess it's both.
I guess it's all of it.

And if you fight so hard for the little moments
it makes you appreciate them more than other—
yeah, I don't want to hear it.
My pain came back after three weeks of bliss.
Three weeks without it. I thought that I was cured.

And still,
there are worse things
than a great life in glimpses.

You are young, in love, and happy—
just a little at a time.

The Bare Minimum

It's easy to forget that some people's bodies
work with them
not against them.

It feels like the bare minimum.
You just want what they have.

Not even a body you loved,
but a body you had a say in.

In Distress

If you smile through it
people will assume
it must not be that bad.

If you cry and scream
and let them know
they'll assume you're exaggerating.

What's the word
for just surviving it?
What if I'm not the hero
or the damsel of my story,
I'm simply in it,
just like everybody else?

Epitaph

Here I am
once again
crushed
by the weight of it:
a body older than I am.

I'd say it never gets better
but that's just not true. It gets better
about as often as it gets worse again.

ANGRY

Medicine Is the Best Medicine

I love those little sayings
about how laughter and sunshine
are the best medicine. Adorable.
Clearly for people
who don't need medicine.
But so fun for them, I'm sure!

And I love when people tell me
that they're also lactose intolerant,
but they eat it anyway
because they just love cheese!
I'm sure you are, I say!
But if I ate that
I would shit clear water!

And I love it when people tell me
they would just die if they had what I have.
It's actually so funny of me
to keep on living.

And the advice, the unsolicited advice!
Mountains of it, especially when I don't ask.
To try yoga and acupuncture
and four different prescriptions
that already failed me
with a little blame
slipped in between suggestions.

And the pressure to be soft
and kind and inspiring always,
even when I'm shitting water.
To be absolutely beautiful
in my ugliness because there's no room
for plain ugliness
without at least a little shine.

Tell the truth but make it sing!
Tell them to stuff their solutions
but with a smile. Comfort other people
with hope about your circumstance
because your naked pain is uncomfortable
to be around.

Be sick but not too much. Be sick
but in a way we understand.
Be sick but make it special!

And look, I guess I like it all a little.
If I'm going to hurt
I might as well get their attention.
I might as well make something good out of it.

And I joke just to survive it. Laugher helps
and probably so does all the rest of it.

But medicine is my medicine.

It's easy to write about all the times they rallied around you. The hospital rooms full of get well soon balloons and cards and flowers and how they drove you to the hospital or held your hand while you woke up from anesthesia. These are the things people want to hear.

But what about the lonely times? The times when everyone else has vacations and deadlines and your disease is just another errand on the day's checklist.

In the movies no one ever shows up at the hospital alone, but in real life you know it happens all the time. You and the other chronic sufferers are parking in the same garage and walking, lonely, up to your appointments. You're nodding when the doctor tells you new risks to your medication and making mental notes to pass along to mom.

And it's always how many years since this surgery and how many years until the next one and the names of all the medications you forgot to memorize because halfway through last year you switched. "I'll have to look that up," and "Let me text my mom," and the mild resentment beating towards all the twenty-five year olds who don't have this down routine.

They send you down two floors and you ride the elevator alone. You take a number and they take your blood like it's the deli and you're what's being served.

And you nod at all the other lonely people, not quite young enough to demand mom fly out for the appointment but not quite old enough to just ask for the company. The people who took the day off work.

They may not have rallied around you this time, but this time you may not have needed them to. You have people to rely on when things get really tough. But when it's just another chore, that's when you rely on yourself.

You are the only one who absolutely has to make time in your daily life for this.

You are the hero here. Balloons and cards be damned.

Lovely

Good good girl
gets her pat on the head, gets her value
from being brave and tough
and bearing the unbearable.
She laughs in the face of
"you shouldn't have to" and says,
no matter, I can stand it!!
The lip is stiff
and the needle is sharp
as she slides her eyes away from the bruise
that blossoms along her veins.
She will make no sound
and be so proud of that,
how tolerable she is,
how gracefully she holds up under horrible things.
She will have the opportunity to cry
and not take it
and then congratulate herself
and resent the ones with fat tears on their cheeks,
how hands flutter to them in the room
but eyes roll behind backs.
She knows, she's seen it,
so she saves her weeping for the car. Compose yourself.
Speak intelligently.
People want to help what they love;
make them love you. Make them love you
and survive
another day.

Ten years old, nine years old,
twenty-five years old, thighs stuck to the paper
and fists balled behind her back.
These are the very first lessons she learns. To be lovely
in addition to everything else.

Of Note

I had a childhood
of doctor's waiting rooms
and trying to describe kinds of physical pain
that I didn't have the vocabulary for.

I had grown men
with medical degrees
dismiss severe gastrointestinal distress
as a tummy ache
because I was a little girl.

I was always either hysterical
or exaggerating my pain
until they cut me open to find the proof
and suddenly I was brave, and sick,
and worth believing.

Nothing had changed
but a note in a chart
and the knowledge
that I could never shut up
until I was better.

And that was how I saved my own life.
The suits were just there,
taking notes.

Monday

All your life doctors tell you how you feel
without ever really knowing.
Everything checks out, they say,
you'll be back in school by Monday!

You call your mom and cry.
I don't know if I can go to school today.
I don't feel well.
And she'll sigh.
"I think you ought to try."

Okay. Okay, I'll try.

Because if there's nothing wrong with you,
like all the doctors say, then why shouldn't you?
All the other kids are trying, and harder than you.
They don't go home in the middle of the day.

It's years before a doctor takes you seriously.
You sit next to your mother
who has taken off work
as he outlines the tests you'll take.
"I'll try anything. I'll try it all."
(It's what you're trained to say.)

Two weeks
and many tests later
he'll tell you that you're fine.

You're fine.

In the car you unclench your fists.
I'm not fine, mom.
I'm not doing this to myself,
I'm not making up my pain.

She doesn't look away.
We will find another doctor, she says.
We will try again.

And you are back in school by Monday.

Happy New Year!

We hung up streamers for New Year's
and now the wall looks blank without them.
Should it?
There was never anything there before.

And nothing's wrong,
just the absence of excitement.
Just every day blank
in front of the other.
Just the people on the internet who say oh god,
doesn't it suck to be scared that you'll get sick
and your immune system won't be able to defend you,
isn't this the *worst*,
it's barely even living,
I can't wait for it to be over in a few months!

And you shut your laptop
like that hasn't been your day to day experience
since college when they told you
Treatment but No Cure.

Some weeks I forget to go outside.
No wonder the walls look blank,
they're not the sky.
My dad says I spend a lot of time on my porch
and I look through my pictures and notice it. I do.
The leaves fell off the tree last month and it was like
vacation—
everything felt so different! Look at all that space!

I wish I had a yard. The leaves made room.

'What's your Covid comfort level?'
the people on the internet say.
'Do you like outdoor dining? It's a personal decision,
everyone feels safe in different ways.'
As if this is about personal comfort. As if
it's a preference.
As if it's about only their safety.

Our choices
affect choices
affect those without choices.
Everyone's life is still a life
whether they have less money
or more or preexisting conditions
or less privilege than you.

The wall's not blank, I have to remind myself.
We just took the streamers down.

Houseplant

We joke that I'm like an orchid—
very hard to keep alive, I guess.
Just the right amount
of water
and sunlight
and even then it's a struggle.

And if I hate my bad health
then I love my good nature.
Sickness didn't plant it in me
like every inspiring story.

It was just always there.
I'd have been a happy and kind healthy person too,
I think.

The Paradox

It goes like this: if you worry about the migraine you will cause the migraine. If you worry about causing the migraine you might cause a stomachache. If you worry about the stomachache you will definitely get a migraine. If you take your migraine pill you will definitely get a stomachache.

The paradox is that every time something good happens I worry about getting sick. Any time there's any excitement on the horizon it is laced with that worry; what if I ruin it somehow, what if I have to miss it, what if I go and am stranded somewhere in pain?

And the worry brings the pain which brings the worry. My first thought when I book the role or get the call back to work or get invited to the party is "what if?" How can I stop my body from taking something away from me? How can I get through something that I'm supposed to be looking forward to?

And sometimes it's so unfair that I just can't take it and sometimes it's just my life so I learn how to adjust. Every good thing has me grateful and worried, fearful and excited. I guess I should expect it by now. I've never felt one without the other before.

Veteran

Other people
get to be afraid
of needles
but I don't.

Fear is a luxury
and my insurance
doesn't cover it.

Patient Was Emotional and Difficult,
She Should Try Yoga

It took ten years
for someone to tell me
"your body is failing you."

Not the other way around.

"Any Allergies I Should Be Aware Of?"

Hi!
I am the stereotype of that
annoying gluten free LA girl!
She is very fun and easy to laugh at
because she is difficult.

We have all seen a movie
where she rattles off her order
very rudely to a waiter
that we are supposed to side with.

I want to say:
when I was younger
I ate my words
instead of food.

When I got to college
and everyone was on a meal plan,
I realized I didn't mind being hungry
if it meant being invited.

I've been called high maintenance,
picky, anorexic. I cannot escape the labels
people like to assign to women.

I would eat before every outing,
alone in my room.

It's a struggle that seems so small
in the scheme of things.
My friends point to a special menu and say
see, it's not so hard!
I don't know how to tell them why it is, though.
I want to say, I watched these movies as a kid.

And then I get angry
that I've called myself dramatic.
And I cry over every time I said
"I'm not hungry."

I was always hungry.
It's such a basic thing,
how could I have thought I didn't deserve to say it?
Everyone deserves
to eat.

The Inverse

They're all so disappointed.
They'll never say it like that, but they are.
Every doctor, every friend, every well-wisher.
They want to see the pay-off of their
positive thoughts and prayers.
It makes for a better story.

Every day that you don't get better
you get more boring and less sympathetic.
As it gets harder for you to bear
everyone around you grows more used to it.

This is the inverse.
You must invent a fresh new way to hurt
or they all get tired of listening.
You must inject a little hope
into the conversation
or watch their attention drift
to something with a more positive outcome.

It feels taboo,
to answer truthfully
when asked how you are.
The one who hates it most is you.
They could never hate it more than you.

The only thing worse than hearing about it over
and over and over again
is living it.

Invisible Illness

I don't celebrate quietly
and I don't suffer quietly.

In a culture where we're taught
to never complain,
I highly recommend
hurting out loud.

The Lesson

When people say
that everything happens for a reason
I don't like it,
but I get it.

And I guess, if I had to say,
I like the person this disease made me into.

But I'm willing to bet, well-meaning
stranger, acquaintance, or friend,
that no matter how much
you admire these traits in me
you would not trade
my patience
for your health.

You would not choose to be
inspiring and wise
in exchange for being sick
and in constant pain.

And if you think I was put on earth
hurt, to teach some big lesson
then listen closer:

because I promise you,
the lesson is not for me.

Price Point

Somewhere in an office
men in suits
who have most likely never suffered from
what I have suffered from
are making decisions about what medications
are deemed necessary
or unnecessary
for my quality of life.

I hope I can afford their complicated view of me.

Repetition

First I call the pharmacy. Same time every week, like I've been doing for years, and they tell me that the price went up or there's a problem with my insurance or that the doctor has to approve the very thing they prescribed me a hundred times already. Then I call the doctor. They put me on hold because she's probably in surgery or out to lunch or getting a hundred calls just like this one, and actually could she email me instead because that's faster? When the email comes through they'll say it was a problem with my insurance. I'll call my mom. She'll call me back. The insurance should actually be fine, sometimes computer systems are slow. Sometimes they have two files for your name. When I drive to the pharmacy the person I'm speaking with will not be the same person from the phone. They will have me wait in two lines to tell me that I should've called. I did! But what they meant is that the medicine is out of stock, I should've called two days ago so they could've ordered it to be here, right now, on the day I have always picked it up for the last nine years. Eventually I will apologize for something. For being complicated, maybe. They will smile and I will smile about what a horrible chore medicine is, and only one of us is being paid to do it. And I will go home with the instruction to repeat it all the next day, and I will, because success of this chore is directly related to keeping me alive. And I might see a friend, if I'm lucky, over dinner at a place where I have called ahead about the menu, and they'll ask what I did today and I'll say "oh, nothing. I almost picked up my pills."

Inspiration Porn

It takes a village to be sick.

Or I should say: it takes a village to maintain my health,
or whatever semblance of it I may have from day to day.

How do you go on when your illness is not
life threatening, just life altering?

When what doesn't kill you
makes you winded after one flight of stairs
and late to every party?

You are now the flaky friend,
the one with debt,
the one who can't move away from their parents,
the one to accommodate.

When you say *this is my limit* they'll coo
and tell you you're so strong.

Sometimes my illness is just a pill I take every morning.

And sometimes it's everything at once.
Every tired saying
they'll never tire of saying
to keep from seeing my frustration.

Please.
The people need an inspiration.

Megaphone

Your pain
is more important
than their discomfort.

You don't choose
when you're in pain,
or when you're sick,
or even the name of your disease.

And if the location of your pain
or the nature of your pain
is making someone else uncomfortable
that's okay--

they are allowed to not listen.

It is not your job to stop talking.

Anger Management

How to manage my anger
at my lot in life
when I know that getting sick doesn't mean
just one sickness, it means all of them.

When friends smile sympathetically and say,
"the flu hit me pretty bad, too,"
but you know it didn't come with a night in the ER
and a vomiting spell and a sinus infection weeks after.

How to remain calm
when the amoxicillin didn't work
but no one will take you seriously until you
finish all ten days of it.
And you wait for the appointment with the specialist
who tells you to wait for a CT scan
and who knows when they'll call?
Meanwhile you have to stay home from work
and wake up every day in pain.
"Soon" takes on a different meaning after that.

Does every doctor know
that they are the fourth doctor you've been to
for the same problem?

Does every eighty dollar copay
know what that adds up to
when you haven't been able to go to work
and you're an hourly employee?

And who else is there at night when you lie
on your bed sobbing?
"I can't do anything, I can't even get well."

Trying to manage my anger
when people say a pandemic isn't a threat
unless you already have something wrong with you,
as if people with illnesses matter less
than healthy people.

Stamping down my anger
because people don't understand that once I get sick
it is the longest, hardest road to getting better.
I haven't been fine in months.

And you can't blame people
for not understanding
what has never happened to them.

You can't blame people because their bodies work
as they should.

You can only explain and hope they try to understand.
They've got no reason to.
You hope they will anyway.

(This is how you manage.)

A Tough Pill:

Being successful
and having an illness
doesn't always mean acting
like that illness doesn't exist.

Questionnaire

Please list any allergies:
any ways you're not the cool girl,
all your high maintenance medical needs
and everything that makes us say aww
as we applaud your boyfriend for putting up with you.

Please list any previous surgeries,
any times you posted a selfie in a hospital bed
to instagram,
anything that will make us roll our eyes and say
she loves all this attention
as we add a heart and tell you how inspiring it is
that you continue existing, a reminder of how lucky
we are for our health.

Please conduct yourself appropriately,
give us access to all medical records but learn
to keep some things *private,* really,
is it so important to discuss this in such detail?
Tell the truth unless it gets unpleasant.

Continue to inspire, suffer prettily,
please refrain from bumming any of us out,
it's for your safety and our comfort that we ask you
to sort these issues out beforehand.

After all, our time is valuable
and you are just another name on a file,
another double tap and box to tick
on our quest to
becoming better people.

Smile now. Be grateful.
Don't worry—
we don't like the word
disabled.

Expert

I wish they didn't expect me
to survive my pain
and be an expert on it,
too.

Chipper, With a Smile

The thought of failure
doesn't do much for me.
Never has. I have been failing since the moment
I stepped onto my own two feet.
Try as hard as I might, I can't get better.
What's a little rejection
when your own body rejects you?
I ease into a situation I'll be bad at.
There are so many things I can't do.
So I'm brilliant and poised
in the face of rejection.
I can take a needle to every inch of my skin—
I can stick the needle in myself.
But I get so mad at the tv. Isn't that petty?
I can't bear to watch people
go to sleep and wake up
not in pain. I can't bear to remember what it felt like
to not have to fight for every moment of rest.
I'm here at the face of another failure.
The stupid part is I did everything right.
I did everything right
but they'll blame me anyway.
I barely tell people anymore,
I'm so tired of seeing on their faces
how it is they justify that I was in the wrong.
I'll come with you, my partner says.
I'll come to every appointment
and tell them you followed the rules.

And if it all goes to hell anyway I'll still be there
and it'll be okay.
He is so sweet and I love him so much.
I want to shake him like the characters on the tv.
I want to say I know it will be okay
because I am the one who has to make it okay.
I will have my moment to cry
and then I will have to pick myself back up
and be positive and schedule appointments
and research all the new meds,
because what else is there, more crying?
My grief is just another thing
that has to get done.
Maybe it's nothing, he says.
Maybe we're jumping to conclusions.
But doesn't he know that the hope hurts worse?
I have been failing in this way all my life;
chipper, with a smile.
And on the best days someone really notices
and says in the quiet:
I couldn't do what you do.
And I smile! Trying and failing all the while.
And I bite back what I want to say,
the obvious, the bitter:

If I didn't have to,
I wouldn't do it either.

The Sum of My Broken Parts

I wish they looked at me
as a whole person,
not a puzzle they have to solve,
my pain an inconvenience
on their way back from lunch.
I wish I was more to them than the organ
bringing down
the sum of my parts.
The faint air of irritation,
the eye roll that accompanies
any mention of another factor of my personhood.
When you bite down the sob and say
"It hurts so bad I can't sleep through the night,"
and the doctor nods politely and tells you
that doesn't fall under their specialty.
I am a good girl
who does all of her paperwork ahead of time.
I am a good girl who arrives fifteen minutes early
and always has her copay
and speaks in a clear firm voice.
I ask the right questions
and only cry when I'm desperate.
I wish they could see what it does
to the good girl who has always minded her parents,
always got A's and people pleased and said yes
to everything anyone asked of her,
how it slices away at the perfectionist girl
to sit on a table and be told over and over
how difficult you are simply for existing.

How keeping your body working for you
is such a problem for everyone.
I don't love medicine, you want to say.
I'm not the person in the room who chose this as a life.
I am the one that it happened to.
Every doctor is so mad
when they see the list of all my surgeries.
I color code it to make it easier. I bring highlighters.
I nod and smile and apologize for being sick.
I am so sorry, always. The attitude,
like it's rude for me to bring up my pain.
Like it's rude for me to push back
and say no, actually that wasn't helping.
It didn't work. Like I'm calling them wrong.
The way it bruises an ego, to believe me.
And I accept it gratefully.
I have no choice. I thank them for their time,
every time. I pay up. I make the next appointment,
put it into my calendar,
make a note to arrive fifteen minutes early.

HOPEFUL

Yours, Alone

Things are bad
but you wouldn't know it.
You limp your way to the appointment,
every light too bright,
every question scrambling in your brain,
impossible to answer.

"What is your pain level?" they ask.
Seven. No, six.
The habit to seem okay is so strong
that it trips you up
even here.

"Do you happen to know the date?" you ask.
The nurse studies you as you fill out the paperwork.
The same information
on three separate forms,
but thinking is so hard right now.
Your pen freezes over the numbers she just told you.
Quietly she repeats the date for you
for every single form.

Things are dire
but they'd never know it.
Pain is your quirky accessory.
You show up to every party
with your head wrapped in cold packs.
I brought the ice!

And everyone treats you like it's perfectly normal—
you suppose at this point maybe it is.
What do you want from everyone?
To know? To act like they don't?
To let you sleep in
but make sure to not have any fun without you?
Please, let them still invite me.

People sometimes don't believe you.
They think if it were really so bad
you'd be home crying in bed.
(They don't see what happens those nights.)
The truth is, on the first day of pain like this
you screamed and thrashed
and rushed to the hospital.
But now it's every day,
so you learned to suffer
alongside happiness.
Because if it came down
between the two, you know
which one is constant.
The other is a choice.

The pain finds you
no matter where you're hiding.
But the happiness? That's yours alone.
You find that for yourself.

Control

You can't control the thing
that is really bothering you,
so you decide to control traffic
instead. It doesn't work,
and you are very late.

The doctor calls
another family ahead of you
and a nurse looks at you
from across the empty waiting room.
"She's taken her second patient," he tells you.
"It'll be about forty-five minutes
until your appointment."

You start to mumble something
about a wreck on the 405
but you choke. No one cares
about the things you can't control.
There has to be someone to blame
for the traffic, and it's not the guy
who got in the accident
or the thousands of people
on their way to work; it is you,
who was twenty-three minutes late.

You are taken to another room for a shot.
A nurse preps your arm and warns you,
"Now we do our best not to make it hurt,
but this is an injection, so you'll feel a little sting."

We do our best not to make it hurt.
We do our best to control the things we can't.
And sometimes your best is twenty-three minutes late
and full of tears. But you're doing it.

The shot does sting,
but you forgive her.
And then you forgive yourself.

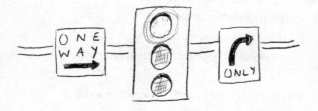

Permission to Rest

Sometimes the only thing worse than the pain
are all the decisions I have to make because of it.

I often wish it were more clear-cut.
I want someone to tell me what to do.
More than that, I want someone to tell me what I don't
have to do.

"You're sick, just rest. What you live with is hard.
Just rest."

But when I weep and complain everyone tells me
that I know how it feels better than they do—
can't they see that that's the problem?
I'm the only one who feels it.

You're sick. Just rest. What you live with is hard.
It's okay to rest.

Silver Linings

The pain doesn't start
with the diagnosis. It starts long before
the flowers
and get well cards
and supportive facebook messages.
Mine started long before
anyone ever called me brave for it.

My diagnosis was the beginning of something
very long and frightening.
But it was the end of something much lonelier.

An Answer as Armor

When you've been in pain
and beaten down
and you think no one will ever understand
to be handed an answer
is to be handed a weapon.

The chance to fight back
after so long of being defenseless.

When Hope is Heavy

I lost something
I thought I couldn't lose.
I'm not where I used to be,
that spot is taken up now.
There are lists of prescriptions
and calls to the companies
that want to take them away from me.
There's the first step out of the doctor's office
when you're trying not to cry.
There's the hope
you pick up and put down.
God, since when is hope so heavy?
I pray. And I take my medicine.
I wish on a star every night
and on the mornings they're still out
when I'm on my way to work.
I shove needles into my legs and neck and jaw.
I do yoga. I do cardio. I swim. I watch the videos
with tricks and hacks and how to clear your chakras
and how to atone for your sins. I listen patiently
when people imply I'm doing something
to deserve it.
I believe in everything and so I try it all.
And I get angry. God, that day I got so angry
that it turned into embarrassment.
I was online reading about what worked for them
and it was everything I had tried already
and I was so, so deep down angry.
Why couldn't I be happy for them?

I had to wait to pick my hope back up again.
Or the time I cried in the car
because I was so nervous about getting to bed on time
and you said you're not alone and I said I know,
but if it goes wrong
you're not the one who has to feel it, I am.
And you held my head in your hands
as we cried at the unfairness of that,
and I said it's so lonely
it's so lonely it's so lonely.
I lost something I thought I could never lose.
My life, as it was before. My head without the pain.
I miss that. It's so lonely.
What do you love the most about me?
Probably your buoyant spirit, you say so quickly.
I laugh at how unexpectedly kind it is.
For a second I see myself
the way you see me:
doing something so impossible every day.
And damn. You got me.
God, I love my life.
There's that hope again.

Hidden Talents

I was trudging through,
as always on my very best behavior,
tripping over disappointments tangled up
like tree roots; fundamental to my very foundation.
But see, I'm good at this—
I never stay down,
my feet never stay still,
my smile never falters. Grief peeks through
on the briefest occasions and I meet it
then leave it behind
because it simply can't keep up.

Oh the effort
it takes to enjoy myself.
I wish they could see how much planning
goes in to every joyful moment. I can do it,
it will just be harder. There will be easy outs
and checkpoints and rescue missions
and if it all goes off perfectly: a moment stolen back.

The pain will take and take and take—
but I have talents, too.

I can steal it back.

Unpause

I have given myself permission
to be happy and be sick
at the same time.

This life hurts.
It hurts everyone in one way or another.
This just happens to be my struggle
right now.

And I have given myself permission
to feel it and still be happy,
and smile, and go on adventures.

I get so tired of always pressing pause.
For now at least,
I want the great big gift of everything at once.

The Magician

I am a very good actress.
I learned from a young age
how to act like I'm not in pain.
Cast me! Hire me! Give me the grade!
Trust me. I can do it. I can be a functioning person,
I can handle the workload, I can go to the party.
Will you be sad if I stay home?
I'm actually feeling better.
Does it hurt? A little.
A smile. One hand distracts
so they don't see what I'm hiding in the other.
It's okay, I'm fine, I'm here,
I comfort, I reassure, I suffer
but I do it so well.
They'd never know unless they read it.
And I can hide it from everyone on earth
except for you.
I wish you knew how much that means to me.
I think I'm being brilliant, hiding,
showing only the best of me.
A perfect execution.
You lean in so no one else can hear,
"it's okay— I can tell it hurts."
The only one who sees
my extraordinary effort. I'm doing great.
You know my secret.
The whole world gets my smile. But you—
you get everything else.

The Errand

Back and forth from the hospital
like it's normal, like it's a chore,
just one check mark on a list
with the date at the top.
Cheek down on the pillow like it's normal,
arms folded, you making chit chat with the doctor
who remembers little details,
a reminder of how often we see her,
and everyone pretends not to notice
the hiccup in conversation
when the needle slides into my face.
"Did the last one hurt?" you ask me when it's over
and I say how did you know?
I've trained my face not to show it.
"I watch your hands," you say. Oh.
I never thought to hide that.
A very long week
with a lot of new pills. Steroids
and then something else. Again,
like it's normal. My weight rises and drops.
I don't feel right in my clothes.
The pain is constant.
Nothing is normal. I want to scream
for everyone's attention. It hurts!
And at the end of it, as always,
another appointment. I cry the whole way
down the elevator. You're startled,
"what's wrong?" you say.

Just all of it, the constant state of it,
the guilt of it, wanting to give you a life
where you aren't carting me to and from
endless appointments, wanting to be the kind of girl
who can be young and carefree,
looking around the waiting room
and seeing how much older everyone is
and feeling like I've lost the best of it already.
Like I never had it when I should have at all.
I don't know how to say it.
Finally: "I don't feel hopeful anymore.
Something always hurts."
So we drive and I weep and you
put on the music that I like. Eventually
I sing along.
I love my spirit— how much it can withstand.
Eventually I mark it off my to-do list.
Another errand down. It fades
into just another part of the day.
The sun is shining and I'm singing
and you'd think it was all perfect
but we know better.
And I'm looking at my hands.
They're holding yours.

Not Lonely

This is the story
of the very bad day
when you couldn't get up off the ground
so the whole family joined you there.

You did your makeup
and picked out the outfit
like an optimist in a fog thinking
if I just keep putting one foot in front of the other
I'll end up in a step without pain.

The keys were in his hand
and your medicine stuck in your throat
and you laid right there on the carpet
without even the energy to cry.

"I don't think I can do it."
All dried up but the tears came anyway.

So you're in pain! You're in pain.
She's not an unfamiliar friend.
You've made a whole life embracing her.

You lay down stubborn, like a child,
thinking about how it's so unfair,
how you don't want to live like this.
But you have to.
Right now this is the life you have.

And your cat crawls onto your tummy.
The one creature on earth
who is not disappointed
when you're sick.
And your partner lies down next to you
and it isn't happy, it's sad. It's still sad
and the pain isn't any better.
But it's something else, too.

On your really bad days
you used to lay on the floor
alone.

Pusher-througher

I have become an expert
at ignoring my pain.
Romanticizing my life
and glossing over the sharp bits
but they snag the picture anyway.

The other day my mom said "you'll push through.
You're the best pusher-througher I know."

I have learned to hold pain
at an arm's length. Sometimes
I can really get a good look at it.
And it's almost always bearable
until suddenly it's not.

I don't show the world because it's ugly
and not hopeful and not inspiring.
I don't show the world because it helps no one.
And still, in between the happy moments
is the compulsion to remind the world that it happens,
even if it's mine, even if I don't want them to see.

Yesterday I asked you who the happiest person
you knew was and you said
"you are."
"Even with everything?" I asked.
Even then.
I'm the best pusher-througher I know.

To Love a Broken Thing

Mine is a body that sometimes lies
in hospital beds.
Sometimes it doesn't take the food
I try to give it.
It is a body that needs shots twice a month
and constant help.
But it is the one that I have.
My body and I have not always been friends.
It has caused me surgeries and pain.
It caused me confusion about what beauty was
when I was at my sickest. But it works.
It hasn't always worked, and now it does,
just enough.
And still I have an illness,
and I always will.
And still I take medication,
and I always will.
And they tell you *"love your body,"*
but mine is constantly changing.
My face changes shape and
sometimes I don't recognize
myself in the mirror.
But I will try
to love my body despite
its inconsistencies
because of the things it holds.
Because my heart
is the one that's inside of it.

A Mini-fridge Full of Syringes

The refrigerated box that your medication is mailed in weighs twenty pounds. You're at your doctor's office, struggling to get a good grip, when the nurse looks at you and asks "You have a car, right? To drive that home in?" For no reason, you nod, and hobble out of the clinic. You have no car. It takes thirty minutes for you and the box to walk home.

The truth of the matter is that you've never given yourself your shots before without help. Yes, you've done it alone once in preparation for coming here, but you had someone on the other end of the phone to coach you through it, and your mom on the other side of a door. And now who knows what time it is wherever your mom is? You draw the blinds and drop your pants.

In the back of your mind you always assumed that you would be forced to stick the needles in your legs someday. But you thought maybe that day was many years in the future, and you'd have to do it alone out of necessity when your kids were at daycare if your husband happened to be out of town.

Instead, you're twenty-one, alone in your room, and you have a syringe in your shaking hand. You tap the bubbles out, sterilize your thigh, pinch the skin, and then slide the needle in. You're growing up in smaller ways than you were expecting. But you are growing up.

Don't Count the Good Days

Back from the dead in record time!
Lost the first few weeks of twenty-nine,
who needs them?

Missed the FaceTime,
texts unanswered. Plans canceled
and then eventually never even made.

Your partner double takes
the first day you're back on your feet.
"It makes me so sad," he says,
"when I can tell you got used to it."

But you're up! You're up. We don't jinx it.

Am I having the best night of my life
or am I coming out of a migraine?

You feel like a kid with their heart broken wide open
for the first time. Every song is louder
and about you specifically,
every joke is the funniest thing he's ever said.

After weeks of a dark room
every moment of normalcy is sensory overload.
We laugh until we cry.

That night we dance to the same four songs
for two hours straight. I think it's both.
I'm coming out of a migraine
and I'm having the best night of my life.

You stand in the middle of the crowd
and grab his face and say
"Is this really how people feel all the time?"
Was I ever really one of them?

But it's yours for tonight.

Don't count the good days.
There's just too few of them.

Write them down and remember them
and hold on as hard as you can.
Chase them down.
Remember that they always come back.

Just don't count them.

Early Onset

My newest medicine
lists a possible side effect
of confusion.
It's not something to laugh about
but I do. I miss the same turn
I always make
and we look at each other and gasp
"is it the new pill?" and as we laugh I think
is it?

I look on the forums
like I always do before possibly
altering my brain chemistry
and everyone is elderly.
People are researching the medicine
on behalf of their aging mothers.
It's supposed to treat dementia,
with a side effect of helping me I guess.
 My treatment is buried under a list of
"you may possibly experience."

I may possibly experience confusion.
May possibly experience dizziness
or difficulty driving. I may possibly experience
relief.

And is it a worthwhile trade? I guess my whole life
is spent in answer to that question.
I'm trading pains for other pains like playing cards.

I'm a collector; I keep myself behind glass.

It's so funny. It has to be funny to be survivable.
And luckily it actually is.

I'm taking risks
and joining forums
for the elderly.
We discuss our symptoms,
weight gain and loss, head fog,
headache. I fight the shooting pains
with a healthy dose of hope
and a larger dose of medicine.
And every time I forgot something I think,
am I sick?
I've made being confused
confusing.
You just can't help but laugh.

Not Tragic

It's not world-ending, just hard.
And sometimes that's the hardest part.
It's only chronic, not tragic.
Chronic pain wears you down the same as any feeling.
I wouldn't mind it once, you think.
I've got doctors in three different parts of the city
and tests ordered by all of them.
I take five different kinds of medication
and tylenol to manage the pain.
And I keep trying to be normal and function
because for now this is just my day to day.
Chronic, they call it.
That's short for "find a way to work through it, kid."
So these are the ways it ruins my life
without ruining my life.
These are the ways it exhausts me,
makes it harder,
leaves just enough room to let me wonder
when I've stayed home if things would've
turned out fine.
And these are the ways I fight it: I still go to the movies.
I leave the theatre when I have to, and then
I slide back into my seat and ask,
hey, what did I miss?
I'm not better, not yet. But I'm trying anyway.
That's a start.

What did I miss?

Again

Our whole lives are cyclical,
if you think about it- you find
and lose people,
you are in love
and you are heartbroken,
you are sick
and you are okay.

And at first it felt unfair, but really,

if every feeling is truly temporary
then I want to feel as much as I can.
I want to keep being sad
and keep being happy.
I want to keep getting worse
and keep getting better.

Again
and again
and again.

Permission to be Great

I wish I could go back in time
and tell that twenty year old
curled up on the hospital bed
that she doesn't need to make it all go away
to have a good life.

It never goes away
and I have a great life anyway.

Good Enough (For Now)

I didn't have a headache
for six days in a row. I can't remember
the last time that happened. Years ago
by now.

I had just started a new medication
and on the sixth day it occurred to me:
I wasn't in pain. I wasn't even worried
about being in pain.

I hadn't taken a rescue medication in a week.
They were packed neatly away in my bag,
forgotten about,
burning a hole
through my insurance's pocket.

I turned to you and said,
with the great trepidation of the very unlucky,
"Am I cured?"

I wasn't.

The migraine after the break was the worst,
not because of the pain
but because of the disappointment.
I went in for my usual treatment
and told the doctor about my little miracle.
"It felt possible to be normal again."

"It is possible," she said.
I made it to the car before I cried.

It's weird, having grown up
with an illness that has no cure.
Doctors tell you we can manage the symptoms
and it will get better
and then probably inevitably worse
and then better again.
They feed you hope in little bite sized pieces,
putting out the fires as they come.
I'm so used to being alright with
good enough
for now.

Sometimes I forget that things can be fixed
forever.
I forget to hope for that.

The World Will Wait

I will not be bowled over.
I will not be trampled.
I will take my time getting better.
And when I am, the world will still be there.
I am a force of nature. The world will wait for me.

Wins and Losses

My pain is so persistent.
Sometimes I feel like it's the only thing
more determined than I am.

I have a good life and I'm missing it.
The guilt is enormous.
I'm terrified that one day I'll look back on my twenties
and they'll be blurry.

Everything is colored by it.
When I look at pictures or think of places
it's the first thing I remember:
whether or not I was in pain.

I guess that's not so rare.
Everyone's fighting something.
Mine just happens to be so obvious.

God I love my life
and I hate that I'm missing it.
I love being myself
but I hate this part of it.

Either I take my medicine and the world is fuzzy
or I don't and everything is so sharp it's blinding.

Progress is hard to take
when it's in years, not months or days.

I have a doctor who really believes me.
I have access to all the best healthcare imaginable.

I have support, money for my medical bills
and a partner who rubs my shoulders
and stands in line at the pharmacy.

I have a group of people listening
with so much love
whenever I complain.

I have a killer sense of humor about it,
all of it. And unlimited optimism,
unlimited energy to fight.
I love that about me.

And I have a headache. Almost always.
Wins and losses wins and losses.

After the Fear Is Gone

It's a strange thing to eat
when you're afraid
that the very food
you are putting in your body
will make you sick hours later.

The hunger doesn't go away.
But the fear eventually gets
much bigger.

I lived ten years
never knowing
if it would get better.

Sometimes you don't realize
how frightened you've been
until after the fear is gone.

(And I stayed afraid. I just didn't let it stop me.)

Secret Weapon

Fight your pain
with kindness.

Kindness wins every time.

Tenacity

You don't cry often
from the pain alone.
Maybe from exhaustion,
or frustration. Maybe, rarely,
you cry from the fear of it:
an illness you can't control.
The worry that a rogue feeling
may not just be a feeling
and might be the start of something more.

But the times you have screwed your eyes
and gritted your teeth
and cried like a child from the sheer pain?
Few and far between.
When you're little and you don't have the words for it,
and when it's hopeless and unchanging
and also, well,
also last night.

You remember all of the times
you screamed from the pain;
easy to count. You remember your father
turning from the room
the first time your mom shot
the medicine into your stomach.
You remember the ambulance,
the morphine that knocked your breath
from your chest,

and the lonely time you drove yourself
to the emergency room in the early dawn.

You remember the pain.

But most of all you remember all the times
you looked your disease right in the face,
saw the terror,
and promised to never let it stop you.

When my migraines first started in February of 2020
I thought they would be over by March.
By March we had bigger problems.
So I crossed my fingers for your birthday, then Easter.
The leaves grew back and I stayed in a dark room
with the shades drawn.
Two medicines tried and failed
and I cried on the couch.
I tried eating more
then eating less then eating clean
and everyone told me to try yoga
so I tried yoga and somewhere in there
I called my mom and told her my goal
was to be better by my brother's wedding
the next April.
She scoffed. Next April?
"I was going to say by the end of the summer."
You iced my face and I wept
through workouts that I was told might help,
I counted down to April,
migraine on my birthday and the day after Halloween
and a new pill that I could only take twice a week
so I rationed,
migraine at work where I pretended I didn't,
proved to myself I could work through it,
cried the whole way home.
Migraine on Christmas Eve but Christmas Day was
perfect.
New doctor, new plan.

"My brother is getting married in April,"
but there's no skipping the waitlist.
I make it to the wedding but part of me does not,
worried about waking up in pain,
worried, being gone even when I'm in the room.
Migraine on Easter,
back to work at the end of April,
migraine at work and I sit in the corner on my break
with my earphones in pretending to read.
New treatment. Thirty needles in my head
and the feeling of getting my life back.
Two weeks in July that I can barely remember.
Steroids and the ER and IV's,
panicked calls to my doctor, another waitlist.
Four weeks off work by the grace of girls
who picked up every shift.
Another treatment.
My life is my life again.
This time you cry. "I just missed you."
Panic attacks when the migraines come back.
"What if it's like last time?" It's not.
But the fear never goes away.
Once it was that bad,
you never stop worrying that it will be again.
And the hope, of course the hope.
Lots of things take longer than you wanted.
Migraine on another birthday.
Crossing my fingers for April.

Happiness as a Form of Rebellion

Chronic pain and
doctor's appointments
have been taking over your days
and it's not that that's new
but this time
you come home
to someone who
loves you.
And it's strange
to suffer and be so safe.
You don't smile through it
for anyone else's sake.
This time your smile is a weapon.

Happiness as a form of rebellion.

Affirmations

I love my body
and forgive
all the ways
it fails me.

A Fighter

I learned to be afraid of food
at ten years old,
when I wasn't getting better
and the doctor suggested an allergy to dairy.

The list got longer
the sicker I stayed.

Out went soda and fried foods.
Still sick. Nothing with coffee or nuts.
Still sick— now nothing
over seven grams of fat per serving.
More tests, more blood,
and still no answers.

By fifteen we had cut out gluten.
And I was hungry all the time:
at the movies, at restaurants,
at sleepovers.
But I was more scared.

I was so good at being hungry and scared.

The fear never fully goes away.
I still get cagey at restaurants.
It's hard to unlearn habits
that spent a decade keeping you afloat.

I will never eat anything
without worrying it will make me sicker.
And I'm not ten years old anymore
and it's certainly not the hardest thing in the world,
but it's hard. And that's okay.

Some fights are big and singular
and make for a great story.
Other fights are small and constant
and we go up against them in little ways every day.

Either way, you're still a fighter.

Prescription

It wasn't until I was there on the floor,
you holding on to me like you could keep me together,
that I realized how hard it's been.
It wasn't until I had any hope
that I realized how long I'd been holding on to smoke.
And I was embarrassed
that I had cried on the phone
until I hung up and you were crying with me.
It wasn't until a doctor looked at me
with a plan to fix my pain
that I realized how resigned to it I had become.
She asked a million questions
and then said exactly what was wrong with me
and I said I know, and we both ignored
that my eyes were bright with tears
for having heard it.
"Here's what we're going to do," she said,
and I fell backwards after the phone call
and I was in pain but I was in pain with a plan,
and for the first time since last April
when it all went to hell
I let myself weep.
Nothing hurt less,
but I could bear it.
It's amazing what a little hope
will do.

More or Less

Life feels very hard right now.
I never asked for more or less.

People always want to know
if I had the option to not be sick,
would I take it?

This is the truth:
the answer is different when I'm in pain.

The experience is awful.
But I value the perspective.

I am feeling everything.
It hurts but I am happy.
I couldn't ask for more or less.

I am learning to celebrate the pain.

How Strange

What a strange,
strange life, to hurt
so badly and still
have everything I need.
What an incredible thing.

Life, the Way it Was Before

I was coming out of my headache
and colors were brighter
and the wind felt divine
and life was so magical
I could've dropped to my knees
and cried.
I could see the relief
on your face, feel your hesitance
to point out that I was among the living
again. Pain is like luck;
you don't want to jinx it.
So I could've wept but I didn't
because weeping causes headaches.
So does drinking, roller coasters,
huge surprises, waking up early
and going to bed late, working out,
getting stressed, relaxing
the moment after the stressful thing passes,
and rain.
I can't control the weather,
so I try to cry less. Sometimes they are
similarly inevitable.
But just then I was happy
and trying not to be too happy.
Trying very hard to live my life
in the middle zone of all feeling
lest I invite the pain to come
creeping back.

It's one of the little tragedies of chronic migraine,
how it robbed me of my glorious indulgent
ups and downs.
This month I had fifteen migraine days.
Ten of them the same headache.
My doctor said after day three
it gets really hard to break. No shit, I thought.
But seriously, when did the trees get so beautiful?
In the week I was in hiding?
You look at me like I'm brand new to earth,
stopping in the middle of the sidewalk
to take a picture
of every pretty thing.
Has life always looked this beautiful? It's addicting,
the saturation, the ecstasy of normalcy.
Everything's in focus
without the distraction of pain.
"My head feels amazing," I say very quietly.
Remember? Don't jinx it.
I could get used to this, I think.
To what, exactly?
Oh. Simple.
Just life,
the way it was
before.

Acknowledgements

Firstly, thank you to Violeta Gavira for bringing my vision for this cover to life. I sent her a photo of my actual messy nightstand and she turned it into a work of art that is so perfectly representative of the detritus of illness. I am so grateful she chose to lend her artistic talents to my little book.

A massive thank you to my friend Nathan. Your patience, humor, and advice are invaluable to me... as is your knowledge of photoshop. You have always come through for me and I have always noticed.

To Kristen and Durbin— thank you for carting me to endless appointments and never making a fuss unless I specifically wanted a fuss made (a hard balance to strike). Your love and friendship has always allowed me to be my sickest, happiest self.

To Elizabeth, who shared an apartment with one chronically ill person and then went on to marry another: thank you for always understanding. And to Chloe, who loved me so much she went out and got Crohn's herself. How's that for loyalty?

Thank you to dodie for championing this book and reminding me that someone may need to read it as much as I needed to write it. To Hope Carew, who filled every prescription with me through college and created a safe space for me (and so many others) to talk about illness in adulthood.

And Dom. Your belief in me is astounding. Your belief in this book nearly broke my heart. Thank you for all the help, edits, formatting, and understanding. All of it. And especially thank you for your illustrations that became the heart of this book. Your doodles, like you, are the best at taking something heavy and making it lighter.

To my mother, my first and loudest advocate: thank you.

And to the doctors that diagnosed me and changed my life, Dr. Bincy Abraham and Dr. Peony Pak: I hope every person who suffers through pain can find a doctor like you. My world was so narrow before you. You have helped me gain my life back.

Finally, to my chronically ill readers, anyone who has reached out to me or found comfort in these words: I have found such comfort in you. This community is the greatest thing the internet brought me. Take your time. You are a force of nature. The world will wait for you.

ABOUT THE AUTHOR

ABOUT THE AUTHOR

Shannon Lee Barry is a writer and actress living in Los Angeles. She is an advocate for invisible and chronic illnesses, and suffers from Crohn's Disease and chronic migraine. For more of Shannon's writing, you can join her @barry_happy on Instagram.